THE PURPOSE EXPERIENCE

DISCOVER AND FULFILL YOUR
GOD-GIVEN PURPOSE

WORKBOOK

TIM WAISANEN

THE PURPOSE EXPERIENCE

ARROWS &
STONES

Copyright © 2022 by Tim Waisanen

Published by Arrows & Stones

All rights reserved. No portion of this book may be reproduced, stored in a retrieval system, or transmitted in any form or by any means—electronic, mechanical, photocopy, recording, scanning, or other—except for brief quotations in critical reviews or articles, without prior written permission of the author.

Unless otherwise marked, Scripture quotations are taken from the Holy Bible, New International Version®, NIV®. Copyright © 1973, 1978, 1984, 2011 by Biblica, Inc.™ Used by permission of Zondervan. All rights reserved worldwide. www.zondervan.com. The "NIV" and "New International Version" are trademarks registered in the United States Patent and Trademark Office by Biblica, Inc.™ | Scripture quotations marked **NLT** are taken from the *Holy Bible*, New Living Translation, copyright © 1996, 2004, 2015 by Tyndale House Foundation. Used by permission of Tyndale House Publishers, Inc., Carol Stream, Illinois 60188. All rights reserved. | Scripture quotations marked **ESV** are from The ESV® Bible (The Holy Bible, English Standard Version®), copyright © 2001 by Crossway, a publishing ministry of Good News Publishers. Used by permission. All rights reserved. | Scripture quotations marked **AMP** are taken from the Amplified® Bible (AMP), Copyright © 2015 by The Lockman Foundation. Used by permission. www.lockman.org |

For foreign and subsidiary rights, contact the author.

Cover design by Sara Young
Cover author's photo by Andrew van Tilborgh

ISBN: 978-1-954089-15-0   1 2 3 4 5 6 7 8 9 10

Printed in the United States of America

CONTENTS

Introduction iv

CHAPTER 1. God's Proposal 5

CHAPTER 2. Pillars Of Purpose 9

CHAPTER 3. The Path To Purpose—Part 1: "Identity" 15

CHAPTER 4. The Path To Purpose—Part 2: "Freedom" 21

CHAPTER 5. Possessed With Purpose 28

CHAPTER 6. The Crossroads Of Purpose 33

CHAPTER 7. God's Purpose Coaching 38

CHAPTER 8. Dare To Dream Differently 45

CHAPTER 9. God's Guidelines For Your Purpose Statement 50

CHAPTER 10. Provision For Your Purpose 55

APPENDIX 1. Freedom Questions 60

APPENDIX 2. Purpose Questions 62

APPENDIX 3. Vision Questions 67

APPENDIX 4. Writing Your Vision Story And Personal Purpose Statement 70

APPENDIX 5. Goals And Plan Of Action 75

INTRODUCTION

Welcome to *The Purpose Experience*! This workbook will be your guide to unlocking the hidden purposes inside of you. The workbook is intended to take you through a life-changing purpose discovering journey. It was developed after a decade of continuing to encounter the same issues with hundreds of young adults who felt stuck and frustrated or just wanted to know what their purpose was. This is a specific and strategic step-by-step process that will help you understand what true biblical purpose is and how to uncover God's purpose for your life specifically. Each chapter's content builds upon the previous one and adds a piece to the purpose puzzle. By the end of this journey, you will write your life purpose statement which will reflect and articulate the reason why God created you.

HOW TO EXPERIENCE THE MATERIAL:

In each section, you will find a **recap** of key themes from each chapter of the book as well as a **video** to go along with the chapter. Begin each section by reading the recap content first, then watch the video to reinforce the material, and end by **reflecting** using discussion questions and/or filling out your individual responses to the questions where indicated. If you haven't read the book yet, then we encourage you to do so as it will help you further understand these concepts. At the end of each section are some reflection and discussion questions. These are meant to get you thinking more deeply and help you process the content either individually or in your group. In the back of the workbook is the **appendix** which contains the personal questions to be filled out individually. These are important and the pinnacle piece of the whole curriculum. In these sections, you will record your answers which will be used at the very end to create your vision story and life purpose statement.

Beware that sometimes this process can be frustrating if the answers don't come right away. Don't worry—just come back later to the questions that seem more difficult as you may need more time to reflect on them. If you find that your answers continue to repeat themselves, that is okay. It is intentional; it will make sense in the end why this is the case. This process is meant to cause you to look inside yourself and wrestle with the deeper questions of life and draw from your experiences to pull out the gold hidden within you.

This workbook is designed in such a way that you can either go through it by yourself or with a group of people. Being that discussion in a group can prove to be invaluable, if you are going through it individually, then consider asking a friend, parent, or mentor to join you either by going through it with you or by simply discussing with them what you are learning after each session. Many times, people learn not just from the material, but also from each other as they process and discuss the content together. Stay open to others' experiences of how they are finding purpose as it can be invaluable and is part of the journey. While you may not end this process knowing exactly what God is calling you to do, you will have a general sense of your spiritual purpose, gain an understanding of how to process your life experiences, and possess a road map to guide you in your purpose journey as you make decisions. It's time to discover the purpose of why you exist! Let's go!

> *"Purpose is experiencing God's process of becoming all you were created to become so that you can intentionally accomplish all you were called to do for His glory."*
> —Tim Waisanen

CHAPTER 1

GOD'S PROPOSAL

READ:

Read Chapter 1: "God's Proposal" in *The Purpose Experience*. After reading the recap, watch the video for session 1. Then, reflect on the questions at the end of this section, and discuss your answers with your study group.

RECAP:

God's proposal is the greatest one that has ever been given. It is the reason we live. To say "yes" to Him is to receive the greatest joy and fulfillment one can obtain.

- Who am I?
- What is the meaning of life—what's my purpose on this earth?
- How do I find my purpose, and how will I know when I've found it?
- How do I know if God is real? How do I know what He wants from me?

At some point in time, each one of us will ask ourselves these age-old questions—the ones that without a relationship with Christ are impossible to answer. We pray that this experience starts to answer these questions and puts you on a path of lifelong discovery of God's ultimate plan for your life. May this process be a model and template which you can refer back to over and over again as you make decisions about what God is speaking to you about your life's purpose in every season of your journey.

> *"The thief comes only to steal and kill and destroy. I came that they may have life and have it abundantly."*
> —John 10:10 (ESV)

God has made us an incredible proposal for living the abundant life if we just follow His plan. But even after we embrace the reality of Jesus as our starting point, we face many difficult challenges of what to do with our lives and how to live out our purpose. God's proposal is an abundant life through a relationship with him. The word "purpose" comes from a root word which means "to propose."

The definition of purpose is the "reason why something exists." Another way to put it is you are a means to an end. This means you were created for a specific purpose. God had a specific intention in mind when He created you. Problems reveal purpose! A cup is for holding liquid, a fork for eating, a refrigerator for keeping things cold. A surfboard is for riding waves. The problem of Goliath revealed David's purpose. We were not created for ourselves but to be a means to an end for someone else.

Many may ask you, "What do you want to do with your life?" However, the right question is this: "What does God want you to do with your life?" Why do you exist? He has made a proposal to you, but will you receive it?

PURPOSE SCRIPTURES:

Jeremiah 29:11-13: "'For I know the plans I have for you,' declares the Lord, 'plans to prosper you and not to harm you, plans to give you hope and a future. Then you will call on me and come and pray to me, and I will listen to you. You will seek me and find me when you seek me with all your heart.'"

Psalms 139:13-14: "For you created my inmost being; you knit me together in my mother's womb. I praise you because I am fearfully and wonderfully made; your works are wonderful, I know that full well." You are not a mistake; you were handmade by God! You were knit together in your mother's womb and specially made for something great!

Ephesians 2:10 (NLT): "For we are God's masterpiece. He has created us anew in Christ Jesus, so we can do the good things he planned for us long ago."

You are not just a work of art; you are literally a masterpiece created by God Himself! You are designed so uniquely that nobody else like you exists.

PURPOSE QUOTES:

"Art was always a means to an end with me."
—Walt Disney

"We make a living by what we get; we make a life by what we give."
—Winston Churchill

"Purpose is experiencing God's process of becoming all you were created to become so that you can intentionally accomplish all you were called to do for His glory."
—Tim Waisanen

REFLECT: (INDIVIDUAL REFLECTION/GROUP DISCUSSION QUESTIONS)

What was your biggest takeaway from this chapter?

___

How does looking at God's offer of salvation as a proposal change your perspective on the message of the gospel?

___

Why is it so important to realize that man's proposals pale in comparison to the amazing proposal God has made to us through His Son, Jesus Christ?

___

After reading this chapter, how would you define "purpose" in your own words? How might it differ from the world's, or culture's, definition of purpose?

___

What's the difference between asking what you want to do with your life and what God wants to do with your life?

How does it make you feel to know that your purpose is already in you—that God has already designed you with it?

In your own words, how does a lack of biblical purpose lead to destruction and despair? Conversely, how is God's purpose fundamental to living a full, abundant life?

What's holding you back from fully saying "yes" to God's proposal?

CHAPTER 2

PILLARS OF PURPOSE

"By staying connected to the source, we gain an unlimited supply of strength to accomplish the very purpose for which we were created."
—Tim Waisanen

READ:

Read Chapter 2: "Pillars of Purpose" in *The Purpose Experience*. After reading the recap, watch the video for session 2. Then, reflect on the questions at the end of this section, and discuss your answers with your study group.

RECAP:

PILLAR #1: PURPOSE IS A PROCESS, NOT A ONE-TIME EVENT

One central truth I've discovered is that purpose is a process, not a one-time event. Purposeful living entails constantly growing and changing. You will evolve and grow for the rest of your life. Here's a truth that reassures many young people I speak to: *You don't have to have everything figured out yet! It's normal to not know what's next. Every season of life has a purpose, and your purpose isn't stagnant.*

Purpose is about the process not the destination. Purpose is about taking intentional steps of faith, each day and in every season of life, that lead to a destination. The end result is that you live out your destiny, having lived a purposeful life.

Many people think purpose is merely doing the things they feel called to do. For this reason, many are dissatisfied with life, even though they have so many blessings. There's always this underlying pressure to achieve more, be more, do more, because we think we haven't "arrived" yet and can't be happy until we do. Then, even once these people arrive at their destination and achieve their purpose, they *still* aren't happy. Why? Because the destination in itself was never the purpose. You have to enjoy the process!

PILLAR #2: TWO MAIN PURPOSES

I believe we all have two main purposes in this life: a primary purpose and a practical purpose. Your primary purpose is permanent and never changes. It's spiritual in nature. Your practical purpose changes from season to season and involves what you're doing presently, day by day. Your primary purpose is your spiritual purpose on this earth. It is eternal. It's all about knowing Jesus and becoming who He has created you to be. Your primary purpose is about your relationship with Christ—being made into His image more and more each day.

Romans 8:29 (author paraphrase with emphasis added) says, "God has predestined [His people] to be *conformed* to the image of his Son."

2 Corinthians 3:18 (ESV, emphasis added) says, "And we all, with unveiled face, beholding the glory of the Lord, are being **transformed** into the same image from one degree of glory to another. For this comes from the Lord who is the Spirit."

God's eternal purpose is to reveal His wisdom to us through Jesus. Ephesians 3:10-11 (NKJV, emphasis added) says, "To the intent that now the manifold wisdom of God might be made known by the church to the principalities and powers in the heavenly places, according to the **eternal purpose** which he accomplished in Christ Jesus our Lord."

Your practical purpose, in contrast, is what you are doing right now, in this present season of life, to make an impact for God. This kind of purpose is temporary—it can change. Practical purpose involves being intentional with life and finding meaning in your current job, school, friends, or other circles of influence. God has you in this present time for a reason. Make the most of it. **When you can embrace your present purpose, you will find joy in the journey.**

PRIMARY PURPOSE	PRACTICAL PURPOSE
SPIRITUAL	NATURAL
PERMANENT/ ETERNAL/ UNCHANGING	PRESENT SEASON/ CAN CHANGE
BEING (WHO BECOMING)	DOING (RIGHT NOW)
RELATIONSHIP WITH CHRIST	RELATIONSHIP WITH OTHERS

PILLAR #3: LIVING A PURPOSEFUL LIFE IS MORE ABOUT BEING THAN DOING

Living with purpose is about being like the person of Jesus before doing the works of Jesus. What we do flows from us being (becoming) the person we are destined to become. Your primary purpose is about being; your practical purpose is about doing. Being comes before, and gives way to, doing. **True biblical purpose means that our being must influence our doing.**

Philippians 2:13 (emphasis added) says, "For it is God who *works in you* to will and act in order to fulfill His good purpose!"

Mark 3:14 says, "He appointed twelve that they might *be with him* and that he might send them out to preach and have authority to drive out demons."

Acts 1:8 says, "Power to *be* my witnesses."

PILLAR #4: YOUR PURPOSE IS NOT ABOUT YOU

Contrary to what the world says, your life's purpose is not about bringing you glory, fame, material wealth, status, or followers. As Ephesians 2 makes clear, you were created to do good works in order to glorify God. Your whole existence and very purpose are to bring glory to God.

Jesus says in Matthew 16:24 that, "If any man would come after me, let him deny himself, pick up his cross and follow me." We must deny the desires and cravings of the world that so many chase after. We must pick up our cross, our individual purpose on this earth, and follow the path Jesus laid out for us. To fail to deny yourself is to divorce from your destiny.

Matthew 16:25-26: "For whoever wants to save their life will lose it, but whoever loses their life for me will find it. What good will it be for someone to gain the whole world, yet forfeit their soul?"

You are called to be a torch carrier! (Video: Story of Brian Marschall—Disney Imagineer)

It's not our job to create our purpose. Instead, we willingly lay our lives down to God, and He reveals it to us! When we surrender and stop trying to figure it all out on our own, we'll discover a cause far greater than any we could have come up with for ourselves.

Purpose is that inner cry that wants to be a part of something bigger than ourselves. It involves having an eternal perspective that takes your focus off yourself and puts it on God. Life is short. We were wired for eternity. Ecclesiastes 3:11 says, "He has also set eternity in the human heart; yet no one can fathom what God has done from beginning to end."

PILLAR #5: YOUR PURPOSE IS ONLY ACCOMPLISHED THROUGH GOD'S STRENGTH

Philippians 4:13 (NLT): "I can do [all things] through Christ, who gives me strength."

John 15:5: "I am the vine; you are the branches. If you remain in me and I in you, you will bear much fruit; apart from me you can do nothing."

1) It is God's strength working in you that provides the ability to fulfill your purpose. If it were obtainable in your own ability, it wouldn't be God. If you can fulfill your life's purpose without God, it's not big enough.
2) Fear paralyzes you and keeps you from pursuing your purpose.
3) Fear puts confidence in your strength, while faith puts confidence in God's.
4) Faith in God's power strips fear of its power!
5) Remaining in Christ is what brings God's strength.

REFLECT: (INDIVIDUAL REFLECTION/GROUP DISCUSSION QUESTIONS)

What concept or principle in this session was the most helpful or stuck out the most for you? Why?

_____
_____
_____
_____

How does it change your perspective of purpose to realize that it's a process, not a one-time event? Does this change the way you feel about your purpose or where you are in your journey right now?

_____
_____
_____
_____
_____

What is God saying to you right now in this season about how you can find purpose? What can you do right now in this present season?

_____
_____
_____
_____
_____

In your own words, how would you differentiate between primary purpose and practical purpose? Why are both essential?

_____
_____
_____
_____
_____

What practical steps can you take to embrace your present purpose right now in order to be content and joyful in the midst of the journey?

_____

_____

_____

_____

_____

Do you struggle to "be" instead of constantly doing? Why do you think our culture is so focused on doing instead of on being?

_____

_____

_____

_____

_____

Why do you think God cares more about the state of your spirit than where you are physically?

_____

_____

_____

_____

_____

How have you already had to deny yourself in order to pursue God's purpose for your life?

_____

_____

_____

_____

_____

How might God be calling you to deny yourself and embrace His plans as you move forward? Don't be afraid to be specific here!

_____
_____
_____
_____

Do you find it tempting to live out your purpose in your own strength or by your own abilities? Explain your answer.

_____
_____
_____
_____

CHAPTER 3

THE PATH TO PURPOSE—
PART 1: "IDENTITY"

"Identity is the foundation of purpose."
—Tim Waisanen

"You can't step into your purpose unless you are living in freedom. You can't live in freedom unless you exercise your authority in Christ. You can't exercise your authority unless you know your identity in Christ. And you can't know your identity until you surrender your life completely to Christ and become His child!"
—Tim Waisanen

THE PATH TO PURPOSE

SALVATION › IDENTITY › AUTHORITY › FREEDOM › PURPOSE

READ:

Read Chapter 3: "The Path to Purpose—Part 1: Identity" in *The Purpose Experience*. After reading the recap, watch the video for session 3. Then, reflect on the questions at the end of this section, and discuss your answers with your study group.

RECAP:

"Identity" is defined as "the distinguishing character or personality of an individual."

Taking on the right identity is key to living out your life's purpose. Identity is the most important topic in this current generation. When you don't know who you are, you begin to take on the identities of others. This keeps you from becoming the unique, authentic you that God created. You'll be hindered from discovering your purpose until you know your identity. **God will not give your purpose to the person you *pretend* to be—He will only give it to the person He *created* you to be.**

Identity gives us the strength to be authentic, take off our masks, and be comfortable in who God made us to be. The higher our sense of identity, the more we realize who we are and whose we are. People who don't have a strong sense of identity lose themselves by living out others' expectations. When your identity and worth are based on what Jesus says about you, others' opinions lose their power. Your self-worth is what helps you cope with life's adversities—it's what gives you the ability to follow your purpose with confidence. Don't let your identity be a copy of someone else's! God has called you to stand out, to take off your mask and discover your true purpose.

> *"Peer pressure is only as strong as your identity is weak."*
> —Tim Waisanen

There are two key parts of identity that we must discover in order to live out our purpose. **Just as there is primary purpose and practical purpose, there is also spiritual identity and personal identity.** Both are equally important—they make up a two-sided coin. The spiritual side of your identity is who you are in Christ; the practical side is how you're wired: your personality, temperament, physical abilities, and so on. Both sides play an integral role in your purpose and how you view and adapt to issues in life.

Personal identity leads to success, while spiritual identity leads to significance.

Success: It is the accomplishment of a desired aim or purpose.

It comes from hitting a goal or gaining wealth, status, influence, and accomplishments.

Significance: It is that inner feeling of fulfillment that your life has meaning.

It's achieved when you use your influence to make an eternal impact on someone else's life.

It comes from knowing how your personal identity fits into God's overall plan to build His kingdom on earth.

Identity is the foundation of purpose. If Satan can steal your identity, he can steal your purpose. This is why your spiritual identity is so essential—because the identity that comes from being in Christ, being citizens of heaven, can *never* be stolen.

Galatians 2:20: "I have been crucified with Christ and I no longer live, but Christ lives in me. The life I now live in the body, I live by faith in the Son of God, who loved me and gave himself for me."

Colossians 3:3: "For you died, and your life is now hidden with Christ."

FOUNDATIONS OF SPIRITUAL IDENTITY:

A NEW CREATION
2 Corinthians 5:17 (AMP): "Therefore if anyone is in Christ [that is, grafted in, joined to him by faith in him as Savior], he *is* a new creature [reborn and renewed by the Holy Spirit]; the old things [the previous moral and spiritual condition] have passed away. Behold, new things have come [because spiritual awakening brings a new life]."

This means that all of our old identity, our past sins, and our old ways of thinking and living are now dead, and we have been resurrected to a new identity and life in Christ with a new purpose.

MADE IN GOD'S IMAGE
Genesis 1:27 (ESV): "So God created man in his own image, in the image of God he created him; male and female He created them."

OUR POSITION AS BELIEVERS IN CHRIST
Our identity in Christ is not about performance; it's about position. We are adopted as His children. Therefore, our identity comes from knowing our Heavenly Father. First John 3:1 says, "See what great love the Father has lavished on us, that we should be called children of God!" Likewise, Romans 8:15 says, "The Spirit you received does not make you slaves, so that you live in fear again; rather, the Spirit you received brought about your adoption to sonship. And by him we cry, 'Abba, Father.'"

- We are adopted as His Children.
- Identity is not about performance; it's about position.
- Spiritual identity comes from knowing our Heavenly Father.

Romans 10:9 (NKJV) says, "If you confess with your mouth the Lord Jesus, and *believe* in your heart that God raised Jesus from the dead you shall be saved!" It doesn't say "Those that behave properly shall be saved." Your behavior will follow your beliefs! When you believe the right things about your life, your behavior will follow those beliefs.

- Right believing leads to right behaving.
- You're not saved by how you behave but by how you believe.

Your identity gives you the ability to exercise your authority and obtain all that God promises you. Our identity is about who we are—our position as God's kids. We have full access to Him through what Jesus did for us! Our identity carries authority. **Authority provides access.** As a child of God, you have every right to access the throne room of God.

If we don't exercise our authority as children of God, the enemy will continue to steal our peace, joy, and purpose.

> *"It is confidence in our identity that gives us the ability to live out God's destiny."*
> —Tim Waisanen

REFLECT: (INDIVIDUAL REFLECTION/GROUP DISCUSSION QUESTIONS)

Why do you think so many in our culture—especially young people—are struggling with their sense of identity?

___
___
___
___
___

Do you find yourself struggling with this issue of identity in any way? How so?

___
___
___
___
___

In your own words, how would you differentiate between spiritual identity and personal identity? Why are both essential?

___
___
___
___
___

What's the difference between success and significance? Where do each have their place in our lives?

___
___
___
___
___

Why is it so important to your identity to realize that you are made in the image of God, and, when you accept Jesus Christ as Lord and Savior, you're adopted as His child?

___

After hearing Karla's story, what stands out to you about her sense of identity? What did she choose to put it in? What did she choose *not* to put it in?

___

How does it change your perspective on identity to know that it's about position rather than performance? Does this change the way you pursue your purpose at all? If so, how?

___

What beliefs do you hold that currently influence the way you behave? Feel free to list some positive, as well as some potentially harmful, beliefs—be honest with yourself! How do you think changing those negative beliefs will affect your behavior and your life in a positive way?

___

How does a person's identity grant that person authority? What's at stake for us if we don't exercise our authority as God's children? What will the enemy be able to do in that situation?

_____
_____
_____
_____
_____

Why is identity so critical to leading us down the path of finding purpose?

_____
_____
_____
_____
_____

CHAPTER 4

THE PATH TO PURPOSE— PART 2: "FREEDOM"

"Knowing Jesus, the Word of truth, eliminates the power of sin over our lives."
—Tim Waisanen

READ:

Read Chapter 4: "The Path to Purpose—Part 2: Freedom" in *The Purpose Experience*. After reading the recap, watch the video for session 4. Then, reflect on the questions at the end of this section, and discuss your answers with your study group. Afterwards, fill out the Individual Freedom Questions in Appendix 1.

THE PATH TO PURPOSE

SALVATION › IDENTITY › AUTHORITY › FREEDOM › **PURPOSE**

To the Jews who had believed him, Jesus said, "If you hold to my teaching, you are really my disciples. Then you will know the truth, and the truth will set you free." They answered him, "We are Abraham's descendants and have never been slaves of anyone. How can you say that we shall be set free?" Jesus replied, "Very truly I tell you, everyone who sins is a slave to sin. Now a slave has no permanent place in the family, but a son belongs to it forever. So if the Son sets you free, you will be free indeed." —John 8:31-36

RECAP:

FREEDOM:

"Once a man has tasted freedom he will never be content to be a slave."
—Walt Disney

So what *is* freedom? Where does it start, and how do we get it? Freedom is a continual state of surrendering control of every area of your life to Christ and being filled with His Spirit to live the life for which you were created. More simply put, freedom is living life as a child of God who is totally surrendered to the Savior.

This is why we spent the previous chapter focusing on identity. True identity gives us the ability to exercise our authority. We're not fighting for victory. Instead, we're enforcing our authority in the world through the truth of the Word of God. This is the fight of freedom; and living a life of freedom is what enables you to step into your purpose.

There are many issues in culture that keep people in bondage. Bondage is anything in your life that has become bigger than God. Both good and bad. The reoccurring general issues that keep young people in bondage are widespread. Many are dealing with fear, depression, anxiety or stress, addiction, worry about the future, finances, health issues, family issues, and so on.

There are two main lies in today's generation that keep people in bondage and prevent their purpose.

The First Lie: I can be my own God.

The Second Lie: I am not good enough.

TEEN AND YOUNG ADULT STATISTICS:

Research from samsa.gov discovered that for young adults ages 18-25:

- 1 out of 7 will need substance abuse treatment at some point.
- 1 out of 10 have thought of ending their lives in the past year.
- 648,000 thousand each year actually attempt suicide.

Barna Research shows:

- 18-24 year olds seek out porn at least once a month and are the largest demographic of internet porn consumers.
- 62 percent of teens and young adults have received a sexually explicit image, and 41 percent have sent one.

Pew research reported:

- In 2017, 1 in 5 teenage girls—nearly 2.4 million—had experienced at least one major depressive episode over the past year.
- The total number of teenagers who recently experienced depression increased by 59% between 2007 and 2017.

Time Magazine reports that, between 2009 and 2017:

- Rates of depression among those ages 14 to 17 increased by more than 60 percent.
- These increases were nearly as steep among those ages 12 to 13 (47 percent) and 18 to 21 (46 percent);
- Rates roughly doubled among those ages 20 to 21.

- In 2017—the latest year for which federal data is available—more than 1 in 8 Americans ages 12 to 25 experienced a major depressive episode.

According to the National Institute of Health:

- 1 out of 3 adolescents between 13 and 18 will experience an anxiety disorder.
- The rate of hospital admissions for suicidal teenagers doubled over the past decade.

Research says that pornography has reached epidemic proportions. According to the Conquer Series, 66 percent of high school boys look at porn once a week.

WALKING IN FREEDOM

There is a flow to walking in freedom. As you can see, there are many issues affecting our culture. What is the solution? How do we break free of bondage? There are some keys we must embrace if we are to walk in freedom.

We must become brutally honest with ourselves and God.

We must get to the root of the problem and not just treat the symptom.

True freedom requires having a truth encounter.

We can't do this until we know the truth. John 8:32 says, "Know the truth and the truth will set you free." It's not the knowledge itself that frees us, but the subject of that knowledge. In John 14:6, Jesus says, "I am the way, the truth and the life. No man comes to the Father but by me." Jesus didn't say He *has* truth, or is *a piece of* the truth. Jesus said, "I am *the* truth!" Jesus is the one who sets the captives free. There is no truth outside of Christ and His word. The power for the believer comes in knowing and choosing the truth.

True freedom comes as we expose the lies we believe and replace them with the truth.

If you want to live out your purpose in freedom, it begins with examining and refining your beliefs. According to Christian psychologist Dr. Neil Anderson, behind every bondage in your life is a lie you are believing.

The ultimate change involves confronting the lies we believe by bringing the Word of God into our situation.

John 1 says that Jesus is the Word. When we bring the Word into our situation, we are releasing the very Source and Person of freedom into our lives! Galatians 5:1 says, "It is for freedom that Christ has set us free." When you invite Jesus into your situation, you're inviting truth and freedom himself!

One of the key lies we must confront and expose is the lie of shame and condemnation.

There is a difference between conviction/guilt and condemnation/shame. Romans 8:1 says, "There is now therefore no condemnation for those who are in Christ Jesus." Shame and condemnation are *not* from God.

Freedom comes from the blood of Jesus.

Ephesians 1:7 (NKJV) says, speaking of Christ, "In whom we have redemption through his blood, the forgiveness of sins, according to the riches of his grace." It is the blood of Jesus that cleanses us and sets us free from the power of sin and death.

Freedom is not the absence of sin but the presence of the Savior!

2 Corinthians 3:17 says, "Where the Spirit of the Lord is there is freedom!" Are there any areas in which you're not walking in freedom? Have you denied the Spirit of the Lord access to any areas of your life? When you allow His presence in, it will bring true freedom. Any area of your life where there is bondage is an area in which you haven't fully allowed the Spirit of the Lord to have control. We have to bring the secret things into the light!

CLOSING THOUGHTS:

The path to purpose is through the doorway of freedom. Finding freedom isn't about performance but about surrendering to the truth of your identity in Christ. It's about bringing all your sins and burdens to Jesus. It's about letting go of your way and trusting in His way. When you embrace your identity in Christ, exercise your authority as a child of God, and walk in freedom, you will be on the path of purpose.

REFLECT: (INDIVIDUAL REFLECTION/GROUP DISCUSSION QUESTIONS)

After discussing these questions with your group or individually reflecting on them, go ahead and get alone with God to answer your own Individual Freedom Questions in (Appendix 1).

_____
_____
_____
_____
_____

How does identity (what we talked about in the previous chapter) give us the authority to live in freedom?

_____
_____
_____
_____
_____

THE PATH TO PURPOSE—PART 2: "FREEDOM"

Tim describes bondage as "anything in your life that has become bigger than God—both the good and the bad." Based on this definition, are you currently in bondage to anything? What is it?

_____

_____

_____

_____

_____

Why is it so dangerous to believe that we can "be our own God"—that we can do this life on our own? Likewise, why is it so dangerous to believe that we're not good enough to fulfill our God-given purpose?

_____

_____

_____

_____

_____

Why is it essential that we're authentic and honest about who we are in order to find freedom? How does this open us up to receive insight from God about our purpose?

_____

_____

_____

_____

_____

What's holding you back from stepping into a life of freedom? What areas of your life continue to grip you, chain you down, and tempt you?

_____

_____

_____

_____

_____

Is it difficult to think of true freedom as full surrender to God? How does our culture combat this with its own definition of freedom?

_____
_____
_____
_____
_____

What do you run to in your time of need? What's your savior? We have to be brutally honest with ourselves here, because until we acknowledge these things, we'll never be able to step into true freedom with God as our only Savior!

_____
_____
_____
_____
_____

Why does Jesus make it absolutely clear that there's only ONE truth? How does this differ from the pluralistic view that's common in today's society?

_____
_____
_____
_____
_____

What lies do you need to replace with the truth of God's Word? Be specific!

_____
_____
_____
_____
_____

Do you tend to feel convicted or condemned when you sin? How can you tell the difference?

How do identity, authority, and freedom impact your ability to live out your purpose?

CHAPTER 5

POSSESSED WITH PURPOSE

"Modern Religion focuses on filling churches with people, the true gospel emphasizes filling people with God."
—A.W. TOZER

READ:

Read Chapter 5: "Possessed with Purpose" in *The Purpose Experience*. After reading the recap, watch the video for session 5. Then, reflect on the questions at the end of this section, and discuss your answers with your study group.

RECAP:

Mark 5:1-20.

They went across the lake to the region of the Gerasenes.

When Jesus got out of the boat, a man with an impure spirit came from the tombs to meet him. This man lived in the tombs, and no one could bind him anymore, not even with a chain. For he had often been chained hand and foot, but he tore the chains apart and broke the irons on his feet. No one was strong enough to subdue him. Night and day among the tombs and in the hills he would cry out and cut himself with stones.

When he saw Jesus from a distance, he ran and fell on his knees in front of him. He shouted at the top of his voice, "What do you want with me, Jesus, Son of the Most High God? In God's name don't torture me!" For Jesus had said to him, "Come out of this man, you impure spirit!"

Then Jesus asked him, "What is your name?"

"My name is Legion," he replied, "for we are many." And he begged Jesus again and again not to send them out of the area.

A large herd of pigs was feeding on the nearby hillside. The demons begged Jesus, "Send us among the pigs; allow us to go into them." He gave them permission, and the impure spirits came out and went into the pigs. The herd, about two thousand in number, rushed down the steep bank into the lake and were drowned.

Those tending the pigs ran off and reported this in the town and countryside, and the people went out to see what had happened. When they came to Jesus, they saw the man who had been possessed by the legion of demons, sitting there, dressed and in his right mind; and they were afraid. Those who had seen it told the people what had happened to the demon-possessed man—and told about the pigs as well. Then the people began to plead with Jesus to leave their region.

As Jesus was getting into the boat, the man who had been demon-possessed begged to go with him. Jesus did not let him, but said, "Go home to your own people and tell them how much the Lord has done for you, and how he has had mercy on you." So the man went away and began to tell in the Decapolis how much Jesus had done for him. And all the people were amazed.

Jesus Wants to Possess You with Purpose.

The dictionary defines "possessed" as "being influenced or controlled by something" (as an evil spirit, a passion, or an idea). The demoniac went from being possessed by demons to being possessed with a new purpose. Jesus wants to give you a new nature, a new identity, and He wants to possess you with His purpose! He wants to birth His plans and destiny inside of you in such a way that your purpose consumes you, and no force in hell can stop you.

ENCOUNTERING HIS PRESENCE:

In order to become possessed with purpose you must encounter the presence of Jesus! Encountering Jesus' presence is about embracing a relationship with Him. Religion is trying to live devoted to God without a living encounter with God! This is why we must fall in love with Jesus. When He touches your life, you'll discover how real He is, and you'll spend the rest of your life wanting to serve him!

> *"Purpose is not a plan. It is a person."*
> —Tim Waisanen

PURPOSE IS NOT A PLAN. IT'S A PERSON:

Purpose isn't found in a program, a plan, a curriculum, or even a bunch of practical how-tos. The demoniac we studied earlier didn't receive his mission first—he encountered Jesus first. Purpose is a byproduct—the overflow—of a Jesus encounter. You can't separate purpose from His presence. There is no purpose aside from Him. The good news is that He promises believers that we will always have His presence: Matthew 28:20 says, "Behold, I am with you always, to the end of the age."

HIS PLANS ARE REVEALED IN HIS PRESENCE:

Everyone quotes Jeremiah 29:11 (ESV): "For I know the plans I have for you, declares the Lord, plans for welfare and not for evil, to give you a future and a hope." However, few quote the most important piece of that chapter, which is verses 12-13 (ESV): "Then you will call upon me and come and pray to me, and I will hear you. You will seek me and find me, when you seek me with all your heart." If you want to be who God is calling you to be, you must prioritize the Person, not the plan. You will find Him when you seek Him with your whole heart. This is the prerequisite to finding His plans because *His plans are revealed in His presence!*

It's when you come into contact with Jesus that you become alive to who you have been called to be and what you have been called to do. In order to find purpose, you must prioritize the Person, not the plan. There *is* no true purpose outside of Christ! In order to become who God is calling you to be, you must make seeking him your greatest priority.

Jesus' presence will birth His purpose in your heart. Find Him, and the plan will be revealed. Diligently seek Him, and He will empower you to live out the reason you exist. It's what happened to the demoniac. It's what happened to me and what I have seen happen to thousands of others. Now, it's your turn. Jesus is waiting for you. Go encounter His presence, and become possessed with purpose!

> *"When we have Jesus' presence, His power automatically comes with it.*
> *His presence empowers you to live out His purpose."*
> —Tim Waisanen

REFLECT: (INDIVIDUAL REFLECTION/GROUP DISCUSSION QUESTIONS)

What thoughts or new insights do you have after reading the story of the healed demoniac in Mark 5?

_____
_____
_____
_____
_____

Why do you think some people are more comfortable with the demonic than the divine? What's potentially challenging about the miraculous work God wants to do by possessing you with purpose?

_____
_____
_____
_____
_____

How can comfort conflict with faith? Where might your own sense of comfort be holding you back from the purpose God has for you to step into?

_____

_____

_____

_____

_____

In your own words, how would you differentiate between God's presence and His power? How are both essential to living out our purpose? (See section regarding God's power and presence in Chapter 5 of the book.)

_____

_____

_____

_____

_____

Why do you think we so often equate purpose with a specific path, plan, or series of steps? What's the potential danger of seeing purpose in this way?

_____

_____

_____

_____

_____

How does it change your perspective of purpose to realize that purpose is a Person? How does this change the way you pursue purpose?

_____

_____

_____

_____

_____

What are some practical ways in which you can "seek first the kingdom of God" (Matthew 6:33) in order to be more presence-driven than purpose-driven? (See section regarding God's power and presence in Chapter 5 of the book.)

_____
_____
_____
_____

Would you say you're currently more focused on your purpose or on God's presence? What makes you answer the way you did?

_____
_____
_____
_____

Where in your daily routine do you need to make space to encounter the presence of God? Make a plan to prioritize this time!

_____
_____
_____
_____

CHAPTER 6

THE CROSSROADS OF PURPOSE

"Discovering our purpose begins with knowing God's priorities and purposes on earth."
—Tim Waisanen

READ:
Read Chapter 6: "The Crossroads of Purpose" in *The Purpose Experience*. After reading the recap, watch the video for session 6. Then, reflect on the questions at the end of this section, and discuss your answers with your study group. Lastly, go to Appendix 2 and fill out your Purpose Questions.

RECAP:
A crossroads is an intersection where decisions are made. Serious, life-altering mistakes can happen. If you make a wrong turn, you can become severely lost or get headed in the wrong direction. You may be standing in the middle of the intersection at a crossroads. You may feel stuck or frustrated, just like I did, and not know where to begin. Or, you may just be looking for what's next. No matter where you are, this chapter is the centerpiece, the heart and soul of this purpose content. Let's get practical, and start bringing it all together.

TAKING INVENTORY
Your purposes are already in you!

Successful businesses take inventory of their products. It's a key part of knowing what sizes, colors, styles, or flavors sell the best—what makes the most money—what's in stock—what needs to be ordered. Taking inventory of your life will help you maximize your life's purpose and live abundantly. How do we do it? By looking at multiple areas of your life in order to gain a clearer perspective and understand what your life offers to the world. This process can be tedious and tiresome, but it's absolutely necessary.

CAREER VS. CALLING:

"Your career is what you are paid for; your calling is what you are made for."
—Tim Waisanen

THE PURPOSE CROSS:

The cross is the most iconic symbol in Christianity. When most people see it, they have an immediate understanding of what it means. A few years ago, God showed me how all the complex ideas around purpose can be clearly applied and communicated through this symbol. These principles of purpose overlay on the cross like a four-way highway. Purpose is found at the intersection of these four paths. They intersect in the middle, right where Jesus' heart was. It is here, in the middle, where God's priorities and our unique design collide! These ideas point to the core purpose of your life.

Each of us comes to a crossroad of decision when it comes to what we want to do with our lives. On the road to purpose, there are signs and mile markers that help point you in the right direction. The Purpose Cross includes your personal identity, practical purpose, and spiritual purpose. As you take inventory of your life, you'll begin to see how each road intersects with the others. These roads meet in the middle—the intersection where "The Heart of God" and "Your Divine Design" collide, causing an explosion of purpose.

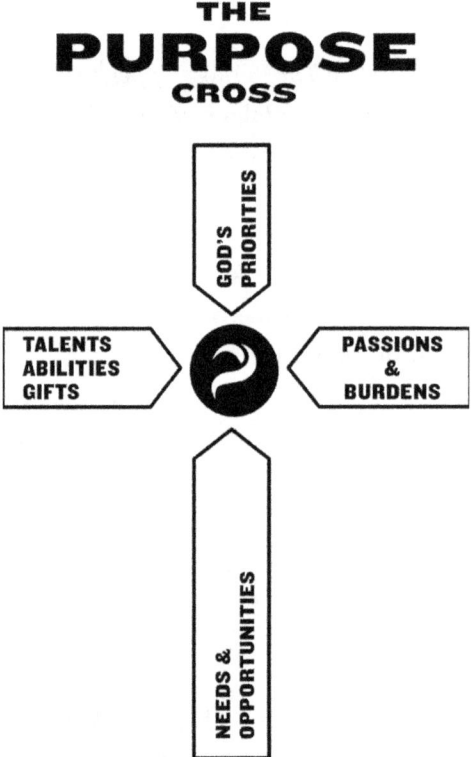

The cross is both vertical and horizontal. The vertical component represents our relationship with God. The horizontal component represents our relationship with others. Both of these are key in fulfilling your purpose. If you don't have both working in unity, your purpose will be incomplete.

"When your career and calling intersect, you are living in your sweet spot."
—Tim Waisanen

GOD'S PRIORITIES ON EARTH:
Discovering our purpose begins with knowing God's priorities and purposes on earth. God already gave us key commands and priorities to live out. We need to ask ourselves some questions: *What's most important to Him? What are His main concerns on earth? What does He want to accomplish?* These are the priorities in heaven that flow down to the earth, to the middle intersection of the Purpose Cross.

The Great Commandment: (love God, love others)
The Great Commission: (make disciples)

NEEDS AND OPPORTUNITIES:
"I didn't realize how one act of obedience could change my destiny. What once was an 'I will never do that' role, became my full-blown passion!"
—Tim Waisanen

Needs and opportunities are God's earthly purposes that He allows you to see. These priorities begin on earth and point us upward toward heavenly priorities—converging at the middle of the purpose cross. If there's a need that keeps resurfacing, even when you've tried to ignore it, it's a clue to your purpose.

T.A.G.: TALENTS, ABILITIES, AND GIFTS:
Talents, abilities, and gifts are those God-given things you're naturally good at. They are things that come easily to us. In *Discover Your Strengths* by Marcus Buckingham and Donald O. Clifton, the authors state that every person is capable of doing something better than the next ten thousand people. They call this area the "strength zone." Working within our talents is key to fulfilling our purpose.

God tags us with spiritual talents, abilities, and gifts when we become born-again Christians. These are the gifts referred to in 1 Corinthians 12. "Giftings," in a spiritual sense, speaks of calling: the spiritual reason you exist and the impact you were created to make. Your gifts give you the ability to fulfill your calling.

"Natural talents are developed through practice; spiritual giftings are developed through prayer."
—Tim Waisanen

PASSIONS AND BURDENS:
Passion is defined as any powerful or compelling emotion or feeling—such as love and hate.

A burden is something that weighs on you—grieves you. It compels you and calls you to take action. What you love and what you hate are two sides of the same coin. They are clues to the problems that God created you to solve. Your passions and burdens provide strength and emotional fuel for your purpose. *Our passions and burdens are shaped by our experiences.*

REFLECT: (INDIVIDUAL REFLECTION/GROUP DISCUSSION QUESTIONS)

What's the difference between your calling and your career? Why are both important?

_____
_____
_____
_____

What's the difference between your job and your career? How do each have their place, depending on the season of life we're walking through?

_____
_____
_____
_____
_____

Take a look at the Purpose Cross diagram again. What are your biggest takeaways when you consider this diagram in light of your own life and purpose? Make some notes below.

_____
_____
_____
_____
_____

What would you say are God's main priorities on earth right now? How do you see Him moving in the world (this could take many forms)?

_____
_____
_____
_____
_____

Where might God be calling you into obedience—to step out, take a chance, love someone, and live out an aspect of your purpose that you've never lived out before?

_____
_____
_____
_____
_____

CHAPTER 7

GOD'S PURPOSE COACHING

"If we want God's results, we must block out the distractions of life and listen to God's voice."
—Tim Waisanen

READ:
Read Chapter 7: "God's Purpose Coaching" in *The Purpose Experience*, to dive deeper into each way God speaks to us and coaches us into our purpose. After reading the recap, watch the video for session 7. At the end, reflect on the questions, and discuss your answers with your study group.

In the game of soccer, there are many voices telling you what to do. There are other players on the field, parents, fans, and even referees. Everyone has an opinion of what you should do with the ball, where to pass, what position to be in, where to run, and how to defend. There are constant decisions to be made on the field. Being a coach, I'm constantly reminding my players that the only voices they need to listen to are the coaches'.

There's one voice we need to listen to: God's. There will be thousands of voices telling you how to live—negative ones, well-intended ones, and misguided ones. If you listen to these voices, you'll miss what God is saying to you specifically. In order for us to pursue our purpose, we need to hear and know the voice of the Lord for ourselves. If we want God's results, we must block out the distractions of life and listen to God's voice.

RECAP:
The goal for this chapter is two-fold: first, that you will see that God has been speaking to you all along, and secondly, that you have a clearer understanding of how God leads you into your purpose.

John 10:2-5 (ESV).

"But he who enters by the door is the shepherd of the sheep. To him the gatekeeper opens. The sheep hear his voice, and he calls his own sheep by name and leads them out. When he has brought out all his own, he

goes before them, and the sheep follow him, for they know his voice. A stranger they will not follow, but they will flee from him, for they do not know the voice of strangers."

Understanding the key ways God speaks to us is critical to recognizing our purpose. His voice gives direction, and direction guides us to our calling.

METHOD 1: HIS WORD
The number one way God speaks to us is through His Word—God's mouth. If your Bible is closed, then so is God's mouth! Just as biology is the foundation to becoming a doctor, so the Bible is the foundation to hearing God's voice.

METHOD 2: HOLY SPIRIT IMPRESSIONS
These are gut feelings, that inner voice of knowing something, or may come like a gentle whisper. Whispers require closeness to hear, reveal God's secrets, and come as a result of intimacy with Him.

> *"Religion yells at you; intimacy whispers to you."*
> —Tim Waisanen

METHOD 3: VISIONS AND DREAMS
God speaks to us in dreams while sleeping, giving us hidden messages, or by giving us a picture in our head, a vision of what He is wanting us to see.

METHOD 4: GODLY RELATIONSHIPS
God also uses relationships to speak to us. These are godly relationships that help us see our blind spots or that confirm God's voice. They may be parents, mentors, coaches, teachers, pastors, other spiritual leaders, or godly friends.

METHOD 5: INNER PEACE
Inner peace is that deep feeling you get when something is right. Even if it makes no sense in your head, or to people outside, true peace is something unshakeable. You know it's from God. God is not the author of confusion but of clarity and peace.

4 KEY WAYS GOD COACHES US INTO OUR PURPOSE
Scripture reveals some key ways in which God coaches us in the process of revealing our purpose. Many times, a combination of the following four ways will be evident. These foundational principles will show up throughout your journey and ultimately lead you to the place God is calling you. These aren't just about spiritual direction; they're also related to the practical components of what you do with your life. As you read through this list, look at your life and see how God has been revealing your purpose. Your eyes will be opened as you realize He's been speaking to you all along!

WAY 1: CALL FROM BIRTH

This is when someone has known their calling since they were young. They always knew God had a specific purpose for them. Many times, this call is validated or confirmed by an adult, parent, pastor, or mentor.

Examples of the call from birth include Jeremiah, who was called to be a prophet to the nations. Jeremiah 1:5 says, "Before I formed you in the womb I knew you. Before you were born I set you apart; I appointed you as a prophet to the nations."

There is also John the Baptist, whose call from birth was to prepare the way for the coming of Jesus. Luke 1:16-17 says, "He will bring back many of the people of Israel to the Lord their God. And he will go on before the Lord, in the spirit and power of Elijah, to turn the hearts of the parents to their children and the disobedient to the wisdom of the righteous—to make ready a people prepared for the Lord."

WAY 2: EPIC ENCOUNTERS

Epic encounters are life-defining times in which God reveals Himself and His purpose supernaturally and specifically. Time seems to stop; His voice becomes clear and undeniable. You know you have encountered God. This communication doesn't have to be in an audible voice or even in a vision. It could be a whisper or a moment when it's undeniable that God is revealing something to you about your purpose.

> Ex: Moses and the burning bush in Exodus chapter 3.
> Ex: Saul's encounter with Jesus on the road to Damascus in the book of Acts chapter 1.

You can have multiple epic encounters in your life. Some may be big encounters; some could be smaller moments in which you knew it was God speaking.

WAY 3: TRYING THINGS ON

Trying things on is one of the main ways God reveals purpose in Scripture and in life. You could say it's like walking through open doors. This concept goes hand-in-hand with the Purpose Cross in how we develop passions and burdens by experiencing them. When we take advantage of the needs and opportunities that present themselves, it is in that place that we do or don't develop a desire for something. Many times, I don't know which direction to go or what decision to make. I find myself praying, "Lord, open the door where you want me, and slam shut the doors where you don't." When a door opens, I go through it and try things on.

Trying things on is like being in God's dressing room: it's a place where you get to see how things fit. Only when you try things on will you know if that outfit on the mannequin looks better on you . . . or if it even fits. How do you know which clothes fit unless you go try them on? You can tell pretty quickly how a pair of jeans or shoes fit: too tight, loose, or just right.

It's in the experience and process of trying things on that one finds what they enjoy, figures out what they are good at, or develops abilities that will be utilized in the future. The doors we walk through often lead us to other doors and to other seasons, where we learn new skills, develop more character, meet new people, walk through new doors . . . and the cycle continues. You end up closer and closer to the place, purpose, and calling God has for you. It's in the process of trying things on that God begins to reveal the reasons why you are where you are and what you need to learn to be ready for your next season. This is all a part of the experience and how God reveals purpose. Trying things on is a big part of the purpose experience. We have to walk down the path of experience in order to grow and find purpose.

Ex: Jesus and the disciples
Ex: Brian Marschall—Disney Imagineer
Ex: Tim's story and journey

WAY 4: SNAPSHOTS

A snapshot is the big picture or general direction God is leading you to go. Way before smartphones and digital cameras, you had to hope and pray that your photographs would come out looking good. You never knew until you developed the film. I even remember using disposable cameras: pointing, aiming, snapping a picture. You'd think you got a great shot, only to have it come back blurry, too far away, or with bad lighting. However, when you got a good photo, it felt rewarding.

When a picture was taken before digital cameras, the light entered the camera, and an image was created on the film. In order for that image to come to life, it had to be taken into a darkroom and developed with chemicals. Over time, it became visible to the eye. You could then print the pictures.

God may give you a vision of the big picture He's calling you to; however, sometimes the details haven't yet developed—they're still fuzzy. You don't know exactly how it's going to happen. You only have a glimpse, a direction, to get you moving. You only have enough information to go off of for your current season of life. This is where we must walk in obedience to what God has revealed to us in this moment, until He shows us the next piece of the puzzle.

A snapshot of your purpose could take the form of an actual vision, a dream, a word God gives you, or just a general understanding of the path He wants you to take. Over time, that picture becomes more and more clear. The longer you live and pursue the things set before you, the more clarity you'll gain about His calling for your life.

Examples:
Genesis 37:6-9 Joseph's dream
Tim's Vision: Go! Be Free! (see video)

The Bible says, "Do not despise small beginnings, for the Lord rejoices in the work to be done" (Zechariah 4:10). We need to be willing to start somewhere. Start small, and watch God be faithful to promote you and breathe upon what you are doing!

> *"All in all, it's not primarily about the vision, but about following the leading of the Vision-Giver."*
> —Tim Waisanen

REFLECT: (INDIVIDUAL REFLECTION/GROUP DISCUSSION QUESTIONS)

What was your biggest takeaway from this session?

___

Would you say that you're fairly familiar with the voice of the Shepherd? Do you find it easy to discern when He's speaking to you? Explain your answer.

___

Which method of God speaking do you hear most clearly? Why do you think this is?

___

Which of the four key ways God coaches us into our purpose has He most used in your life specifically? Is there more than one?

___

How does the idea of "trying things on" take some of the pressure out of pursuing your purpose? Why do you think we rarely give ourselves permission to take this approach?

_____

_____

_____

_____

_____

Have you "tried on" any paths, jobs, careers, or other directions and decided they weren't for you? What were they, and what did you learn from that experience?

_____

_____

_____

_____

_____

What "snapshots" have you received from God as it pertains to your purpose? How did these give you a better idea of where He may be leading you?

_____

_____

_____

_____

_____

Did the analogy of the "darkroom" help you understand God's hand in revealing your purpose in any new ways? If so, what are they?

_____

_____

_____

_____

_____

As you finish this chapter, what action steps do you believe God is leading you to take?

_____
_____
_____
_____

CHAPTER 8

DARE TO DREAM DIFFERENTLY

"God has put a vision inside of you, even if you can't see it yet! He sees things in you that you don't yet see yourself."
—Tim Waisanen

READ:
Read Chapter 8: "Dare to Dream Differently" in *The Purpose Experience*. After reading the recap, watch the video for session 8. Reflect on the questions at the end of this section, and discuss your answers with your study group. Then, go to Appendix 3 and fill out your Vision Questions.

RECAP:
Proverbs 29:18 (AMP): "Where there is no vision [no revelation of God and his word], the people are unrestrained; But happy and blessed is he who keeps the law [of God]."

What is vision? How do we get it, and where does it come from? Vision is defined as "the act or power of seeing or imagining something." Vision is the big picture in your mind of what you want to accomplish. It's the ability to imagine and visualize a desired outcome. It's seeing the end result, outcome, or impact of something you want to do. Once you have vision, you can work towards a goal.

Vision involves seeing what others don't.

On October 1, 1971, five years after the great Walt Disney passed away, Disney World held its grand opening for the Magic Kingdom. During the dedication ceremony, one of the executives turned to Mrs. Disney and said, "Isn't it a shame that Walt didn't live to see this?"

Mrs. Disney replied, "He did see it—that's why it's here!"

Vision focuses on the end result, goal, or impact.

Walt Disney said, "A good ending is vital to a picture, the single most important element, because it is what the audience takes with them out of the theater." We stated earlier that vision is about the big picture ending. So I ask you this: What does the movie of your life look like? When your life comes to a close, what do you want those in the audience to walk away with? What do you want to be known for? What do you want your life's legacy to be? We see clearly the impact of Walt's life and vision. What about yours?

FINDING A BIBLICAL VISION

"True vision is having God's perspective about our lives and the world in which we live."
—Tim Waisanen

True vision comes from God and leads to purposeful living. Without a vision, we walk around lost—just surviving instead of thriving. We lose hope and slowly drift away from God. However, when we get a vision, we begin to live the abundant life for which God created us.

Proverbs 29:18 says, "Where there is no vision people perish, but he that keepeth the law, happy is he."

- —Amplified Bible (AMP): "Where there is no vision [no revelation of God and his word], the people are unrestrained; But happy and blessed is he who keeps the law [of God]."
- —New Living Translation (NLT): "When people do not accept divine guidance, they run wild. But whoever obeys the law is joyful."
- —God's Word Translation (GW): "Without prophetic vision people run wild, but blessed are those who follow God's teachings."

The word "vision" in Proverbs 29:18 is the Hebrew word *châzôwn*. It refers to a divine vision, dream, or revelation. Without vision, people die inside. They lack purpose. This leads to boredom, boredom is the breeding ground for an idle mind, and an idle mind is the devil's playground. Proverbs 29:18 shows that having no vision will cause a generation to run wild, be unrestrained, lack self-control, and decay. God must reveal what He wants us to do, or we will run wild and perish!

THE POWER OF PERSPECTIVE:

To get clarity about God's vision, His point of view, we must get His perspective—we must come higher and get closer to Him to see what He sees. Isaiah 55:9 (NLT) says, "As the heavens are higher than the earth, so my ways are higher than your ways and my thoughts higher than your thoughts." Seeing things God's way will help us see beyond the obstacles and challenges, the excuses and fears, beyond all the unknowns and uncertainties.

Hope in the Lord gives you true, biblical vision. Hope is illustrated through the picture of an eagle in Isaiah 40:31: "But those who hope in the Lord shall renew their strength; they will mount up with wings as eagles; they will run, and not be weary; and they will walk, and not faint." Many times, life beats us down, and we lose hope, which leads to a lack of vision. The storms bring doubt, fear, and disappointment. We wonder why God is allowing this to happen. Unless we go higher in our perspective, we won't be able to see the purpose in it all. Hope in God gives you panoramic vision—a vision that's colorful, clear, and beyond your natural ability. Our victory as Christians lies in our getting God's perspective. Once we do that, we can see the vision and the future that He has for us.

YOUR SIGNIFICANCE AND DIFFERENCE:
Your significance is hidden in your difference. Find your difference, and you will find your purpose. A key to finding purpose is discovering the vision you're passionate about and fulfilling it differently than anyone else. What separates you from someone else? What makes you different?

Being different requires being authentic. God's anointing flows through your authenticity! Don't try to be just like someone else; don't succumb to the pressure to be bigger than anyone else. Be the best version of you that you can be. Be the best *you* God created! The anointing—His power on your life's vision—comes through being authentic.

> *"People without vision try to be like everyone else."*
> —Tim Waisanen

STEP 1: NARROW YOUR FOCUS
What is your brand? What do you want to be known for? Most people are known for *one main thing* they did on this earth. When I say names like Michael Jordan, Lionel Messi, Paul McCartney, George Lucas, Jennifer Lopez, Steve Jobs, Elon Musk, Martin Luther King Jr., Billy Graham, or Tiger Woods, what comes to mind? Usually, there is one main thing they're known for.

Narrowing your focus makes it easier to say "no" to things that distract you from your vision. Let your "yes" become so big and clear that it becomes easy to say "no."

STEP 2: FIND YOUR GIFT AND MAKE IT BETTER
Once you know what you're good at—what your gift is—work on it to become the best version of yourself you can be!

Examples include the Disney Principle: Take what you are already doing and make it better. Do it better than anyone else. And Tim's Story: from a youth *generalist* to a youth *specialist*.

Proverbs 18:16 (author paraphrase) says, "A man's gift will make room for him and will bring him in front of prominent men."

> *"You are a gift to the world. What you do with your life is your gift back to God!"*
> —Tim Waisanen

GET A VISION FOR YOUR LIFE:
We must get a vision for our lives. Joel 2:28 and Acts 2:17 say, "In the last days, God says, 'I will pour out my Spirit on all people. Your sons and daughters will prophesy, your young men will see visions, your old men will dream dreams.'" Joel 2:28 uses the Hebrew word *chizzâyôwn* for vision, which means "expectation by dream." When we are in His presence, He will pour out His Spirit and put His dreams into our hearts. Get your heart ready, and ask with expectation for Him to reveal His vision for your life!

At the end of your life, what will people say about you? What will they thank you for the most? How is your life an answer to other people's needs and prayers? What are you doing that causes heaven to come down to earth? Consider this statement as it relates to your life:

When I am doing _____, heaven comes to earth and has an impact on others.

REFLECT: (INDIVIDUAL REFLECTION/GROUP DISCUSSION QUESTIONS)

HOW TO FIND YOUR VISION

The key to this session lies within the practical application of HOW to find your vision. This session is the starting point in helping you discover the vision God has for your life. Discuss the reflection questions, then go to Appendix 3, and by yourself answer the vision questions. Take your time, and let the Holy Spirit help you dig deep into what the vision for your life is.

How would you define vision in your own words after reading this chapter?

_____
_____
_____
_____

How does faithfulness to your <u>current</u> practical purpose pave the way for stepping into your future vision? What does this look like practically in your life right now, today?

_____
_____
_____
_____
_____

Why is it so essential that our vision lines up with the truths of God's Word?

How does a lack of vision lead to discouragement, despair, and destruction?

What do you see in your vision that others don't see? What difference or unique perspective may be the key to discovering your significance?

An inauthentic life is a life without purpose. In what ways do you want to be more authentic as you step more fully into your purpose? (Remember, inauthenticity includes trying to be like somebody else!)

CHAPTER 9

GOD'S GUIDELINES FOR YOUR PURPOSE STATEMENT

READ:
Read Chapter 9: "God's Guidelines for Your Purpose Statement" in *The Purpose Experience*. After reading the recap, watch the video for session 9 and then discuss the reflection questions with your study group. Lastly, go to Appendix 4 and complete your Vision Story and Purpose Statements.

RECAP:
Jesus had a few different purpose statements:

Luke 19:10 (NKJV): "[I have] come to seek and save that which was lost."

1 John 3:8 (AMP): "The Son of God appeared for this purpose, to destroy the works of the devil."

Luke 4:18-19: "The Spirit of the Lord is on me, because he has anointed me to proclaim good news to the poor. He has sent me to proclaim freedom for the prisoners and recovery of sight for the blind, to set the oppressed free, to proclaim the year of the Lord's favor."

When we take God's visions and dreams for our lives and create a practical plan, they will produce purpose. Purpose brings hope! Hope is what gives you a reason to hang on. It gives you something to focus on—the good things, the possibilities of what God created you for—instead of focusing on the negatives and problems all around you. You focus on what you can do and not what you can't do. You see opportunities, not obstacles. The result is hope! This concept is what purpose is all about.

In this session, we will work on pulling everything together. This is where your spiritual and practical purpose comes together and takes shape. It is in this process of creating your vision story and purpose statement that your purpose really comes alive. Walt Disney said, "Dreams, ideas, and plans not only are an escape, they give me purpose, a reason to hang on." He knew that taking one's dreams and creating a plan was a powerful principle that provided purpose! This is the escape route that offers hope and will rescue you from living a boring life.

A vision story is a broad, general description of what you see yourself doing. Your vision story can be anywhere from a few paragraphs to two pages.

Your purpose statement is a more concise, boiled-down theme derived from your vision story.

GUIDELINES AND PRIORITIES:

God's First Guideline: The Great Commandment:

Mark 12:30-31 (NLT): "And you must love the LORD your God with all your heart, all your soul, all your mind, and all your strength. The second is equally important: 'Love your neighbor as yourself.' No other commandment is greater than these."

Loving God and others will lead you to your purpose. In order to write our statements, we must first look at God's priorities. We unpacked these in the "Crossroads of Purpose" chapter. God's first priority on earth for us is twofold: to love Him and love others. This is the Great Commandment of Mark 12:30-31.

God's Second Guideline: The Great Commission:

> *Jesus came and told his disciples, "I have been given all authority in heaven and on earth. Therefore, go and make disciples of all the nations, baptizing them in the name of the Father and the Son and the Holy Spirit. Teach these new disciples to obey all the commands I have given you. And be sure of this: I am with you always, even to the end of the age." —Matthew 28:18-20 (NLT)*

Everything we put energy into should somehow impact others by showing them the love of God. This is the purpose and mission of the church. It's our personal mandate as well. No matter what purpose we live out, at the core, we are to make disciples.

HEBREW PURPOSE:
CHESED: Acts of loving-kindness

Biblical purpose is simply having a relationship with Jesus so that He can begin leading you to bless others. The most important thing in blessing others is the concept of *chesed*. It's the one and only thing that supersedes the *Shabbat*, or "Sabbath,"—that is, a day of rest, a day to do no work of any kind. The highest form of *chesed* is giving to the poor; it also encompasses helping a neighbor or friend with an important need, whether physical, emotional, or spiritual. *Chesed* is taught in Judaism using the principle that, when you are serving others, you are serving God! It is a form of worship. That's why Jesus says in Matthew 25:40 (author paraphrase), "Whatever you do unto the least of these, you do it unto me."

Our purpose and vision must demonstrate God's priorities—and that includes showing loving-kindness. Otherwise, it's not biblical purpose, and it won't be fulfilling—to us or to those we serve.

CORE VALUES:

ALIGNMENT DETERMINES ASSIGNMENT: "CORE VALUES"

"Our core values determine our choices which determine our destiny."
—Tim Waisanen

Core values are personal beliefs that guide your decision-making. The core values you align with determine who you become—and that determines the assignment God will entrust to you. Your core values steer your life, family, and career. They are the values and principles you hold deep in your heart. They are the "brand," the non-negotiables, of your life. Your core values will be reflected in your vision story and purpose statement.

Examples of core values:

Purpose: to live intentionally and fulfill the purpose God created me for
Integrity: to be a person of integrity and honesty
Passion: pursue the things I am passionate about and inspire others to do the same
Relationship: prioritize having deep, meaningful, and life-giving relationships
Faith: to live with a bold and radical faith in God that has a supernatural impact

WRITING YOUR VISION STORY AND PURPOSE STATEMENT
*Your vision story and purpose statement should reflect the truth that your reason for existing is to solve a problem in a way that demonstrates God's love for humanity.

In order for your statements to be complete, they should:

- Reflect and incorporate God's eternal purpose and priorities on earth (great commandment and commission)
- Solve a problem by addressing a need
- Represent your passions
- Include your personality and the way you are wired (personal identity)
- Utilize your talents, abilities, and gifts (practical purpose)

EXAMPLE OF A PURPOSE STATEMENT
NICK, in 2013 as a high school senior:

"I want to use my gifts of teaching and problem-solving to impact communities and aid those in need by creating and bringing solutions. I also have a passion for training people in the Word, resulting in disciples who make disciples."

GOD'S GUIDELINES FOR YOUR PURPOSE STATEMENT

NICK, in 2020: *(Nick went from a high schooler questioning his faith to working in real estate development and serving as a high school soccer coach.)*

"To use my gift of teaching and problem-solving to impact my soccer players and colleagues. To influence others for the eternal kingdom of God through stewarding real estate and business assets. To utilize my passion for training people and players in the theological nature of the Word and building relationships with them, resulting in disciples who make disciples."

Nick is an example of how a purpose statement can grow over time as you go through God's process of finding and developing your purpose.

Consider these additional questions as you write your vision story and purpose statement:

- How can I take the vision of my life and merge it with God's purposes and priorities?
- What is God already doing and breathing upon in our world, and how can I join in this?
- How can I become effective at making disciples no matter what my current practical purpose is?

REFLECT: (INDIVIDUAL REFLECTION/GROUP DISCUSSION QUESTIONS)

*After listing your five core values and reflecting on the discussion questions, go to Appendix 4 and complete your vision story and purpose statement.

List here your top 5 core values (see above for examples) and put a brief description of what the word/phrase means to you:

1) _____
2) _____
3) _____
4) _____
5) _____

DISCUSSION QUESTIONS:
Why is the first guideline, the Great Commandment, essential to your vision and purpose statements?

_____
_____
_____
_____

Why is the second guideline, the Great Commission, essential to your vision and purpose statements?

_____

_____

_____

_____

In your own words, how would you explain how these guidelines work together as guardrails for your vision story and purpose statement?

_____

_____

_____

_____

How does the idea of *chesed,* "acts of loving-kindness," affect how you look at your purpose?

_____

_____

_____

_____

CHAPTER 10

PROVISION FOR YOUR PURPOSE

"God is the source of all provision. All our needs are met through Him."
—Tim Waisanen

READ:

Read Chapter 10: "Provision for Your Purpose" in *The Purpose Experience*. After reading the recap, watch the video for session 10, and then discuss the reflection questions with your study group. Lastly, take a look at Appendix 5 and write down some quick goals and plan of action to move forward today!

RECAP:

Philippians 4:19: "And my God will meet all your needs according to the riches of His glory in Christ Jesus."

PROVISION #1—PROVISION THROUGH PEOPLE:
People are a key piece to becoming who God has called you to become and accomplishing what He has set before you to fulfill.

Ex: Friends, family, mentors, pastors, coaches, business leaders, or even online influencers.

The first way God makes provision for your purpose is through people. On the other side of the coin, one of the main destiny destroyers of your future is found in your relationships. Many young people get on fire for Jesus, find purpose, but then get sidetracked—due to a significant other or close friends. Show me your friends, and I'll show you your future. You will become like those with whom you hang out. Who are your closest friends?

Find people who have vision and passions similar to those you have, and hang around them. These are the men and women who encourage and provoke you to pursue your dreams simply through their presence. Surround yourself with those who are like-minded.

Another way God makes provision through people is by giving you mentors and coaches in life. These are invaluable people to have as you pursue your next season of life. Joshua had Moses. Elisha had Elijah. Timothy had Paul. And the disciples had Jesus. God puts in your path people who have more life experience than you and who can help you improve, excel, and see your blind spots. They can also help open doors of opportunity for you!

PROVISION #2—PROVISION THROUGH YOUR WORDS:

If you haven't done so, read this section in the book in its entirety. It may be one of the most critical teachings on purpose for young adults you've ever heard.

The greatest power we possess is in our tongue. Words plant seeds into our present that provide a harvest in our future. When the Bible speaks of words, or the tongue, it is talking about our profession—the way in which we openly declare our beliefs, faith, and opinions. Proverbs 18:21 (author paraphrase) says, "In the power of the tongue is life and death, and those that love it will eat its fruit." We have the ability to speak either life or death over our lives. Our words will either build us up or tear us down. You will eat the fruit of what you speak. You'll either be filled with a harvest of faith to fulfill your purpose or with doubt and fear. You decide what words come out of your mouth!

Our words create our world! One of the main ways we're made in the image of God is in our ability to speak. God spoke, and the earth was created. When we speak, things are created. Our speech shapes our emotions, thoughts, and actions. We talk ourselves into things and out of them. Our words will create an environment where our purpose will grow or die.

> *Avoid godless chatter, because those who indulge in it will become more and more ungodly. . . . In a large house there are articles not only of gold and silver, but also of wood and clay; some are for special purposes and some for common use. Those who cleanse themselves from the latter will be instruments for special purposes, made holy, useful to the Master and prepared to do any good work. Flee the evil desires of youth and pursue righteousness, faith, love and peace, along with those who call on the Lord out of a pure heart. Don't have anything to do with foolish and stupid arguments, because you know they produce quarrels.*
> —2 Timothy 2:16, 20-23

In this charge to Timothy, Paul makes a comparison between "special purpose" and "common purpose." Another version calls it "noble purpose." Noble purpose leads to grace and honor, while common purpose leads to dishonor, shame, and disgrace. The path of common use and purpose is the one most of society takes. Living for a special and noble purpose is the path less taken and requires our words being filled with life—not godless chatter.

The word "godless" comes from the Greek word *bebelos*, which means "profane, worldly, or common." It's where we get our English word "profanity." This gives the picture of someone walking down the common, ungodly, and profane paths of culture.

The word "chatter" comes from the Greek word *kenophonia*. It has two root words: *kenos* and *phone*.

Kenos means "empty," the absence of good and, therefore, contains the presence of evil. *Phone* means "voice, language, sound, tone, or to articulate." Chatter is therefore, empty, evil language.

When you combine them, the words carry the idea of the battle between the holy and unholy—good and evil—*profane and purposeful.* "Godless chatter" represents brainless activity, wasting your time, and doing nothing productive. It's perverted speech that comes out of our mouths: speech that is twisted, lacks God, and is full of man's wisdom.

Godless speech is much broader than negative words—it's void of God altogether!

The key to stepping into your God-given purpose resides in your mouth. What you speak will either prevent or propel you into your purpose. God has a special purpose for your life; qualifying for it is contingent upon your willingness to line up your words to God's Word. Cleanse yourself from and remove empty, profane, aimless, negative, critical, godless speech!

> *"If you want to step into your destiny and purpose, take the path that's different from the common path of the world."*
> —Tim Waisanen

PROVISION #3—PROVISION FOR YOUR PRACTICAL NEEDS:
God is your source; man is a resource. This is a concept that came to me in prayer one day, and I have built my ministry on it. We cannot look at man as our source. God is the creator and source of all provision. However, He chooses to use people as a resource to provide for our purpose. The Bible says in Luke 6:38, "Give, and it will be given to you. A good measure, pressed down, shaken together and running over, will be poured into your lap. For with the measure you use, it will be measured to you." There are people out there who are watching your life that have the ability to bless you or open doors for you beyond what you can imagine!

One of the greatest ways God will reveal Himself is in the way He provides for your purpose in practical ways. Philippians 4:19 (author paraphrase) says, "My God shall supply all of my needs according to his riches in glory." As I previously shared, Matthew 6:33 echoes this truth. Jesus said to "seek first his kingdom and his righteousness, and all these things will be given to you as well." God will provide for where He guides. When you put God first, you align yourself with all of heaven's resources.

REFLECT: (INDIVIDUAL REFLECTION/GROUP DISCUSSION QUESTIONS)

How has God already made provision for your purpose through people? Whom has He brought into your life to provide opportunities, encouragement, support, and wisdom?

_____

_____

_____

_____

_____

What do your current relationships indicate about your future? Are there any ways you want to grow in this area?

_____
_____
_____
_____
_____

How can you seek out mentors and coaches in this season of your life? Do any people in particular come to mind?

_____
_____
_____
_____
_____

What kind of world are your words creating? Do you tend to speak more positively or negatively—with more faith or more fear?

_____
_____
_____
_____
_____

In what ways do you need to change the words you're using—both internally and externally—to speak about yourself and your purpose?

_____
_____
_____
_____
_____

In your own words, how would you differentiate between special purpose and common purpose?

How has God used trials and challenges to refine you and lead you further into your purpose? What have you learned about yourself and about God through these experiences?

In what ways has God provided financially for your purpose? How have other people partnered with Him in this area of provision?

As you finish this study, what action steps do you believe God is leading you to take? What are your main takeaways, reflections, next steps, and thoughts?

APPENDIX 1

FREEDOM QUESTIONS

1) What has been the biggest struggle for you this past year?

_____
_____
_____
_____

2) What "experiences" or events in your past have caused you the greatest pain? Describe how you felt and how they've impacted you?

_____
_____
_____
_____

3) What areas of your life continue to be a struggle for you and hold you in bondage? These are the areas where you are most prone to sin. They hold you back from God and from feeling His total freedom. (They could be cycles of sin that repeat, emotions, etc.) Why do you think these are still an issue?

_____
_____
_____
_____

4) Are you holding onto any unforgiveness or bitterness towards anyone? If so, whom and why?

_____

_____

_____

_____

5) What were the important things that you didn't receive from your parents or people around you while growing up that you wish you had received? (Examples include guidance, support, positive words spoken to you, physical affection, etc.) Write down what those general things were (if any) and what phrases or words you wish you had heard.

_____

_____

_____

_____

6) What things were you glad you did receive while growing up that have impacted you?

_____

_____

_____

_____

7) What needs to happen or change for you to be able to walk in total freedom right now? How would it affect your life immediately, and what would it mean to your future?

_____

_____

_____

_____

APPENDIX 2

PURPOSE QUESTIONS

Fill out these Purpose Cross questions. Take your time, and be thorough.

GOD'S PRIORITIES:
What are God's priorities on earth? What is most important to Him?

_____
_____
_____
_____
_____
_____

What do you see that God wants to accomplish on this earth right now that lines up with these priorities?

_____
_____
_____
_____
_____
_____
_____

NEEDS AND OPPORTUNITIES:

What are the biggest needs you see in our world right now? (general/big-picture needs)

_____

_____

_____

_____

_____

What needs do you see in front of you that you have the ability or desire to meet?

_____

_____

_____

_____

_____

What opportunities are available to you right now? Or, are there any opportunities that continue to present themselves to you, even if you try to ignore them? (These could be opportunities to volunteer/serve, get a job, take more schooling, or gain new experiences.)

_____

_____

_____

_____

_____

TAGS: (TALENTS, ABILITIES, AND GIFTS)

What do you enjoy doing? What kinds of hobbies and interests do you have or what are some things you really love to do?

_____

_____

_____

_____

What natural talents, abilities, and gifts do you possess? What are some things you do better than most around you and are "naturally" good at?

_____
_____
_____
_____
_____

What produces the most fruit when you do it? There is no denying that when you do these things, you get results. (Don't disregard anything; just write it down.)

_____
_____
_____
_____
_____

What are some things that others validate about you and recognize you for? What things do you do that people compliment you about? When you are doing _____, people notice and admire you for it.

_____
_____
_____
_____
_____

What have been some of the greatest achievements in your life? Things you have done or accomplished that you are most proud of?

_____
_____
_____
_____
_____

PASSIONS AND BURDENS:

What are you passionate about? What do you love to do? What energizes you?

_____
_____
_____
_____
_____

What do you love to do that makes the world a better place or in some way contributes to and adds value to the lives of others?

_____
_____
_____
_____
_____

What things make you lose track of time when you're doing them?

_____
_____
_____
_____
_____

What do you daydream about?

_____
_____
_____
_____
_____

What do you hate? What burdens weigh upon you? What grieves you? Things you hate to see, injustices that fire you up, and things that stir you to take action!

_____

_____

_____

_____

What life-changing experiences have made a deep impression on you? Both positive and negative experiences. How have they impacted you?

_____

_____

_____

_____

APPENDIX 3

VISION QUESTIONS

If you could do anything in the world, you couldn't fail, and money wasn't an obstacle, what would you do? What would you attempt or pursue for God?

_____
_____
_____
_____
_____
_____

If everyone got paid the same hourly wage, no matter what job they did, what would you want to do?

_____
_____
_____
_____
_____
_____

What is it that you do differently than anyone else? How do you do it uniquely?

_____
_____
_____
_____

What do you do that causes heaven to come to earth and impact others?

_____
_____
_____
_____
_____

When you close your eyes and dream of the kind of life and impact you want to have, what do you see?

_____
_____
_____
_____
_____

What does the video/movie trailer in your mind look like? Describe what you are doing and where you are. Who are you with? What impact does it have? Whom is it impacting?

_____
_____
_____
_____
_____

Most people are known for one thing they did in this life! What do you want your legacy to be that you leave on this earth? What is that ONE thing you want to be known for?

_____

_____

_____

_____

_____

What part of God's priorities on earth do you see as being most important to you—The Great Commission and The Great Commandment. How can you align your vision with these priorities?

_____

_____

_____

_____

_____

How can you narrow your focus and become better at what makes your dream different? What do you need to say "NO" to or let go of?

_____

_____

_____

_____

_____

APPENDIX 4

WRITING YOUR VISION STORY AND PERSONAL PURPOSE STATEMENT

KEY PHRASES AND THEMES INVENTORY:

- Go back and read through all the questions from Appendices 1, 2, and 3.
- On each one, take inventory of all the *key words*, *phrases*, and *themes* used in your answers by circling the ones that are either important to you or are repetitive.
- Now, list each one of those phrases and themes below.
- Every time you see a phrase used again, make sure you write it down below.
- After making your long list, go back over it and circle the ones that are repetitive.
- Then, next to those you circled, write the number of times that word, phrase, or theme was used.

Key Phrases and Themes: (LIST BELOW)

_____
_____
_____
_____
_____
_____
_____
_____

MY VISION STORY:

After reading through the key phrases and themes you listed, take these running themes and use them to write your Vision Story. It can be a few paragraphs or up to two pages that pull everything together and share the essence of what you feel God is calling you to do with your life. This is a narrative that tells the themes and story of your life, kind of like a movie trailer describing what you are doing, whom you are doing it with, what people you are impacting, what the impact is that you are having, and the result of your doing these things. It is what you want your life to look like.

Don't get overwhelmed. This is a rough draft, a brainstorming exercise to get you thinking and one step in moving toward your purpose. This can change over time, and you can add to it as you go. However, this will at least get you thinking about what is most important and the type of impact you want to make.

My vision is . . . AND . . . I see myself doing . . .

_____
_____
_____
_____
_____
_____
_____
_____
_____
_____
_____
_____
_____
_____
_____
_____
_____
_____
_____
_____

MY PURPOSE STATEMENT:

In one concise paragraph, share why you exist—the problem you were created to solve. This may be a general spiritual purpose at first and will grow over time as things become clearer.

My life's purpose is to . . .

_____

_____

_____

_____

_____

_____

_____

_____

_____

_____

_____

_____

APPENDIX 5

GOALS AND PLAN OF ACTION

It has been said that a dream or goal without a plan is just a wish. To get you moving towards your purpose, take a moment to <u>write down</u> some basic goals as well as a plan of action to accomplish them. This is not meant to be a comprehensive goal setting plan but just a general starting point. You can get more specific and detailed as you grow in clarity of what you want.

My 30-day goals are:

_____
_____
_____
_____
_____
_____
_____
_____
_____
_____
_____
_____

My 90-day goals are:

_____
_____
_____
_____
_____
_____
_____
_____
_____
_____

My 1-year goals are:

_____
_____
_____
_____
_____
_____
_____
_____
_____
_____

APPENDIX 5 - GOALS AND PLAN OF ACTION (SUGGESTED FINAL EXERCISE)

My 5-Year Plan:

This includes bigger picture ideas. List what you want to accomplish and who you want to become. Examples include graduate college, start a business, find a new job/career, get married, go into ministry full-time, etc. Think about the person you want to be in the future, and start doing the things that kind of a person would be doing right now!

_____

_____

_____

_____

_____

_____

_____

_____

_____

_____

_____

_____

_____

_____

_____

_____

_____

_____

_____

_____

_____

_____

www.ingramcontent.com/pod-product-compliance
Lightning Source LLC
Chambersburg PA
CBHW080547090426
42734CB00016B/3224